5

Green

Verde (VEHR-day)

The body of a man surrounded by piles of jade, a beautiful **green** gemstone, was uncovered in the jungles of southern Mexico in 1952. The man wore a jade mask on his face and a jade ring on each finger. He was found in a tomb inside an enormous pyramid called the Temple of the Inscriptions in the ancient Maya city of Palenque. The man, who had been dead for more than a thousand years, was Lord Pacal, the ruler of the Maya in the seventh century.

The Maya were a group of Indians who thrived in Mexico from about 300 B.C. until A.D. 900. They were an advanced people. The Maya developed their own system of writing. They also had an understanding of astronomy and mathematics that was ahead of their time.

Colors of MEXICO

by Lynn Ainsworth Olawsky
illustrations by Janice Lee Porter

Carolrhoda Books, Inc. / Minneapolis

For Duane, with love and gratitude—LOA

To my friend Maria Elizabeth Xóchihua Strickland and to her wonderful children, Crystal, Raquel, Rebecca, Bryan, and Gabriela, these pictures are dedicated with gratitude and love—JLP

Map on page 3 by John Erste

Copyright © 1997 by Carolrhoda Books, Inc.

This book is available in two editions:
Library binding by Carolrhoda Books, Inc., a division of Lerner Publishing Group
Soft cover by First Avenue Editions, an imprint of Lerner Publishing Group
241 First Avenue North
Minneapolis, MN 55401 U.S.A.

Website address: www.lernerbooks.com

Library of Congress Cataloging-in-Publication Data

Olawsky, Lynn Ainsworth.
  Colors of Mexico / by Lynn Ainsworth Olawsky ; illustrations by Janice Lee Porter.
    p.   cm. – (Colors of the world)
  Chiefly in English with a few words in Spanish.
  Includes index.
  Summary: Explores the different colors found in Mexico's nature and history.
  ISBN 0-87614-886-0 (lib. bdg. : alk. paper)
  ISBN 1-57505-216-4 (pbk. : alk. paper)
  1. Mexico—Juvenile literature. 2. Colors, Words for—Juvenile literature.
[1. Mexico. 2. Color.] I. Porter, Janice Lee. II. Title. III. Series.
F1208.5.063   1997
972—dc20   96-42523

Manufactured in the United States of America
4 5 6 7 8 9 – JR – 06 05 04 03 02 01

North
America

Atlantic
Ocean

Mexico

Central
America

South
America

Pacific
Ocean

Sierra Madre Occidental

Sierra Madre Oriental

Mexico

Gulf of
Mexico

Cozumel

Yucatan
Peninsula

Paricutín
Volcano ▲

Tenochtitlán ●

☆ Mexico
   City

Angangueo ●

Pacific Ocean

Sierra Madre del Sur

Palenque ●

El Chichón ▲
Volcano

Introduction

Mexico is a land of great
contrasts. It has fertile farmland,
tropical rain forests, arid deserts,
and snowcapped mountains. Visitors
can explore the ruins of cities more than
a thousand years old and the modern streets of Mexico
City, one of the largest cities in the world.

Mexico lies south of the United States and north of Central America. It is about the size of Arizona, Colorado, New Mexico, Okla-
homa, Texas, and Utah combined. The country's official language
is Spanish, although many Indian languages are still spoken there.
Most Mexicans are related both to the Indians who were the first
people to live in Mexico and to the Spaniards who conquered them.

3

White

Blanco (BLAHN-koh)

White skeletons decorate houses and shops throughout Mexico on El Día de los Muertos, the Day of the Dead. The Day of the Dead is actually a three-day festival during which people remember loved ones who have died. The festival starts on October 31 and ends on November 2.

The Day of the Dead may sound like a very sad holiday, but it's really a lot of fun. Mexicans visit markets filled with sweets and toys for the celebration. There are gaily decorated sugar candy skulls and *pan de muertos* (bread of the dead), a bread with bone-shaped decorations. Children try to frighten each other with skeletons that pop out of tiny toy coffins.

The last day of the festival is spent in the cemetery. Families picnic on the favorite foods of those who have died and decorate the tombstones of loved ones with flowers and candles. In the evening, the cemetery glows with the light of hundreds of candle flames.

7

Orange

Naranja (nah-RAHN-hah)

There is a place high in the peaks of the Sierra Madre Occidental, near the town of Angangueo, where the trees are covered with brilliant **orange** butterflies every winter. There are so many butterflies that the branches creak under their weight. The butterflies are monarchs. They migrate to this spot in the mountains from Canada and the northern United States each year, traveling in groups of thousands. One year, people figured that there were fourteen million butterflies in an area the size of three football fields. The monarchs spend the winter in Mexico, resting and escaping the cold, before heading north again.

Blue

Azul (ah-SOOL)

Pirate ships once sailed the **blue** ocean waters surrounding the Mexican island of Cozumel. Cozumel lies twelve miles off the coast of the Yucatan Peninsula. During the 1600s and 1700s, the island was a perfect hideout for pirates. Not only was Cozumel deserted at that time, but it also had many ancient tunnels, dug by the Maya Indians, that could be used to hide treasure. Pirates would attack passing ships and steal their cargo, sometimes sending unlucky sailors to the bottom of the sea.

In modern times, Cozumel has become a favorite destination for tourists. Visitors from around the world enjoy scuba diving and snorkling off the coast of the island. Divers who know of Cozumel's colorful past keep a lookout for sunken ships. There's no telling what treasure is hidden under the sea.

11

Brown

Café (kah-FAY)

A home for a Mexican family could be an apartment in a high-rise building made of steel or a modern house made of wood, but many Mexicans live in houses made of **brown** adobe. Adobe is a mixture of clay, straw, and water. This mixture is molded into bricks and left to dry in the hot sun. The adobe bricks are used to build walls, which are then plastered with a layer of mud or clay. Thick walls of adobe help to keep a house cool under the hot Mexican sun.

13

14

Yellow

Amarillo (ah-mah-RIH-oh)

Yellow corn tortillas are served at almost every Mexican meal. Corn tortillas are flat, round pieces of bread made from corn flour. At breakfast, corn tortillas might be served with eggs and refried beans, all topped with chili sauce. At dinner, a large meal served in the middle of the afternoon, or supper, a smaller meal eaten later in the evening, corn tortillas might be part of a main dish. Tacos are a popular Mexican dish made by folding a corn tortilla around a filling, such as beef or chicken. Enchiladas are corn tortillas wrapped around a filling—such as meat and cheese—covered with a spicy sauce, and baked. Corn tortillas are even used instead of silverware to scoop up food, or as a plate held in the palm of the hand.

Black

Negro (NEH-grow)

A church tower sticking out of a **black** lava bed is a dramatic reminder of what happened to the Mexican village of San Juan Parangaricutiro. With an explosion of ash and gases, Paricutín Volcano pushed its way out of a cornfield in 1943, growing hundreds of feet in only a few days. When the volcano erupted, it buried eleven villages in lava, burning-hot melted rock. The volcano has been quiet since 1952. About a billion tons of lava poured out of Paricutín Volcano during the nine years it was active. Paricutín is not Mexico's only volcano. It lies in an area just south of Mexico City that has seen the eruptions of many volcanoes, including El Chichón in 1982.

18

Red

Rojo (RO-ho)

Gleaming piles of bright **red** chili peppers are a common sight on market day in Mexico. In the country, people buy their fruits and vegetables from open-air markets, and chilies—the ingredient that gives Mexican food its mouth-burning taste—are almost certain to be on the list. Shoppers walk from stand to stand, often stopping to greet a friend, as they compare the goods on display. When the perfect fruits or vegetables have been chosen, perhaps the firmest, reddest chilies, a shopper will bargain with the seller until a price is agreed upon and the sale is made.

19

Gold

Oro (OH-ro)

Greed for treasures of **gold** brought Spanish conqueror Hernán Cortés to Mexico. In 1519, Cortés and his men marched on the city of Tenochtitlán, which was the center for the powerful Aztec

Indians. The Spaniards had been told that the city was overflowing with gold and other riches.

At Tenochtitlán, the Spaniards captured Montezuma, the leader of the Aztec Empire. Montezuma was kept captive in his own city, and later he was killed. The furious Aztecs attacked the Spaniards. Cortés and his men grabbed as much gold as they could carry and tried to escape from the city. The Aztecs trapped the Spaniards at the edge of a lake, and the Spaniards had to drop their treasure and swim for their lives. Cortés later conquered the city and brought the Aztec Empire to an end.

Purple

Púrpura (POOR-poor-ah)

You can look in almost any direction from almost any place in Mexico and see mountains, **purple** in the distance. Mountains cover more than three-fourths of Mexico. Three of the country's great mountain ranges are called the Sierra Madre, or Mother Range. In the east, running parallel to the coast of the Gulf of Mexico, lies the Sierra Madre Oriental. Western Mexico is home to the Sierra Madre Occidental. These mountains stretch an incredible two thousand miles, from just north of Mexico City all the way up to Arizona and New Mexico, and have canyons that are deeper and longer than the Grand Canyon. To the south, bordering the Pacific coast, is the Sierra Madre del Sur.

23

Index